A Char

Story and pictures by
Jill Glassco

Deep Sea Publishing, LLC

Copyright Page

The sale of this book without a front cover is unauthorized. If this book is sold without a cover, then the author and the publishing company may have not received payment for it.

A Chancellor Ferry Tale, Copyright © 2016 by Jill Watson Glassco

Cover design: Ben Glassco

All rights reserved. Published in the United States by Deep Sea Publishing LLC, Herndon, Virginia.

This is a work of fiction. Names, characters, places, and incidents either are the product of the author's imagination or are used fictionally. Any resemblance to actual persons, living or dead, events or locales is entirely coincidental.

No part of this publication may be reproduced, stored in a retrieval system, or transmitted in any form by any means – electronic, mechanical, digital photocopy, recording, or any other without the prior permission of the author.

All rights reserved solely by the author. The author guarantees all contents are original and do not infringe upon the legal rights of any other person or work. No part of this book may be reproduced in any form without the permission of the author.

All Scripture passages are taken from the New Living Translation (NLT) of the Holy Bible or the King James Version (KJV).

New Living Translation copyright © 1996, 2004, 2007, 2013 by Tyndale House Foundation. Used by permission of Tyndale House Publishers Inc., Carol Stream, Illinois 60188. All rights reserved.

The Holy Bible, King James Version. Cambridge Edition: 1769; King James Bible Online, 2016. www.kingjamesbibleonline.org.

Printed in the USA

ISBN-13: 978-1939535344
ISBN: 1939535344

www.deepseapublishing.com

Table of Contents

Chapter 1: Send Me 1
Chapter 2: Ready, Set 7
Chapter 3: Go! 14
Chapter 4: Peter 19
Chapter 5: The Club 25
Chapter 6: Prayer Pals 32
Chapter 7: On the Farm 37
Chapter 8: Peter's Burning Question 43
Chapter 9: Cumulonimbus Picnic 49
Chapter 10: Well Done 55
AFTERWORD 62

For my twelve children and grandchildren:

Rebecca and Stephen

Easton Jacob

Anya Elizabeth

Fisher Isaac

Ben and Gabbi

Colton Alexander

Liam Hunter

Dan and Mandy

Elijah Lee

You are treasured gifts from God above - deeply loved and prayed for every day.

"I could have no greater joy than to hear that my children are following the truth."

(3 John 1:4 NLT)

Chapter 1
Send Me

"Look, Papaw," said Jacob, "a walking stick."

Mr. Willowkins and his oldest grandson studied the skinny, brown bug clinging to a porch post.

"That's a praying mantis, Jacob," said Mr. Willowkins. "See the bent front legs? Looks like it's praying, doesn't it? Humm…front *leg* rather. This poor fellow's missing a limb."

Mrs. Willowkins stopped rocking baby Lee. "Missing a leg?" she said. "Is it the right one?"

"Yes, ma'am," Jacob answered.

Mrs. Willowkins chuckled. "Well, bless my stars and garters. Another five-legged mantis after all these years."

Elizabeth saw the twinkle in her grandmother's brown eyes and stopped pulling the wagon and little Alexander around and around the wrap-around porch. "I think Mamaw has another story to tell," she said.

"Oh, boy," said Isaac.

"Boy!" mimicked little Alexander.

Behind the Willowkins' hunting cabin, the Coosa River flowed silently under a full moon's glow. Bullfrog croaks, cricket twitters, and firefly winks in the warm summer evening painted a picture-perfect backdrop for storytelling.

Wilbur Willowkins and twelve children and grandchildren gathered around Martha Willowkins. Two years had passed since their unforgettable summer with Mr. Greenleaf at the big house over Blue Heron Lake, and two more wee-Willowkins had joined the family: baby Lee and baby Hunter, little Alexander's new brother.

"Well, children, long, long ago in eighteen hundred and ninety-two," began Mrs. Willowkins, "a fellow named John "Praying" Hyde sailed across the ocean blue to the far-away land of India. In the depths of India's Punjab, the hard-of-hearing missionary labored throughout the villages from sunup to sundown - praying fervently for lost souls to escape the devil's clutches and run into the everlasting arms of God.

And lo and behold, as grace would have it, the Lord answered Hyde's prayers in a powerful way and snatched hundreds from the flames of judgment."

"But this story isn't about Praying Hyde, the missionary," she continued. "Tonight's tall tale, flavored with an ample portion of truth, is about a praying *bug* – yes, a little, brown mantis named Norman Hyde that lived alongside Alabama's Coosa River during the Great Depression of the U.S. of A."

"Mamaw, what does a missionary in India have to do with a bug in Alabama?" asked Elizabeth.

"I'm glad you asked, sugar. The story's told that on a hot July day in the little town of Childersburg…"

Norman Hyde climbed the whitewashed siding onto a windowsill beside the Estey pump organ - his regular seat on any given Sunday at the Mt. Olive Missionary Baptist Church. A peak inside found a middle-aged man in a worn, black suit leaning over the pulpit. Rivulets of sweat streamed down his furrowed brow. A number of menfolk lined the hardwood pews, mopping their faces with white handkerchiefs, and womenfolk fanned their red-cheeked babies. The blistering summer heat of 1935 felt hotter than sizzling grease in a frying pan, and a breeze through the open windows was about as rare as pocket change in the offering plate.

Americans, in those days, struggled to keep their heads above the fierce economic typhoon, and folks in the south – Alabamians in particular – were hit harder than a Babe Ruth home run. With daddies out of work and families out of food, a single egg became so valuable that a farm boy could trade it for all the candy he wanted at Dunlap Grocery and Market out on Highway 91, and I reckon, in some ways, the bug-kind got by better than mankind. At least they could catch supper instead of having to grow it or buy it.

Not all bugs had it so easy, though. As a youngster, Norman, unwise to the hazards of human-folks, had lost his right foreleg in a slammed screen door on Mrs. Adkins' back porch and was pitched headlong into the School of Hard Knocks. He soon learned that single-legged meal trapping was pert near unmanageable, and simple things like walking through tall grass or creeping up a church wall took him twice as long as the other little mantises. And to make matters all the worse, instead of being sympathetic to his dilemma, the local bug-boys poked fun at his awkward prey-catching and called him "Preyless" Hyde.

Because his slowness made him customarily tardy, by the time Norman reached the windowsill, Pastor Titus was concluding the morning message. The preacher pounded the podium with his fist and bellowed, "Beloved, we may be troubled on every side, but we refuse to be distressed."

"Amen!" shouted Norman, but the humans didn't seem to notice.

"We may be cast down, but we will *not* be destroyed," the preacher thundered. "Yes, like the Apostle Paul, we know what it's like to go hungry, but whether in lack or abundance, we *can* do all things through Christ who strengthens us! Men and women, boys and girls..."

And bugs, thought Norman.

"Poverty must not paralyze God's people from taking the hope of the Gospel – the Good News of Jesus – to a hurting world. As the prophet Isaiah heard the cry of the Lord the year King Uzziah died, oh, people of God, hear His voice calling today, 'Whom shall I send, and who will go for us?'"

Norman volunteered quicker than an American Revolutionary minuteman. He waved his front leg enthusiastically and cried, "Here am I; send me!"

REFLECTIONS

POINTS to PONDER

1. Pastor Titus said, "Hurting people need to hear the Good News of _____."
2. When the preacher said, "Who will go for us," Norman said, "Here am I; send _____!"

God's PROMISE to you:

"Therefore, go and make disciples of all the nations, baptizing them in the name of the Father and the Son and the Holy Spirit. Teach these new disciples to obey all the commands I have given you. And be sure of this: I am with you always, even to the ends of the age." (Matthew 28:19-20 NLT)

(Hidden PEN POINT)

(TITUS- was one of Paul's converts who accompanied him on his 3rd missionary journey and later served as a young pastor in Crete. The book of Titus in the New Testament is a letter that the Apostle Paul wrote to him.)

(Read Titus 1:1-5)

Can you find the hidden PEN POINT in chapter 2?

HINT: The hidden PEN POINT will always be something from the Bible.

Chapter 2
Ready, Set...

"Mamaw, are you making this up?" Isaac asked.

"Shhhh," said his mother. "Just listen to the story, buddy."

Mrs. Willowkins winked at Isaac and smiled. "Eager to go on mission," she said, "a mere four minutes after his arrival..."

Norman started for home as fast as his five legs would carry him. Since mantises never build nests or hives and normally live on trees or bushes or any camouflaging plant findable, the little bug had lived his entire life beside the church in a lavender crepe myrtle tree - with the exceptions of one afternoon's disastrous venture next door to Mrs. Adkins' back porch and, of course, his routine Sunday visits to the windowsill. To save time, the insect took a shortcut underneath the church and scuttled through thick dust.

"Where you going in such a big rush, sonny?" called a crackly voice from a dark corner. "Is your house on fire?"

Norman paused for his five eyes to adjust to the dim light.

"*Five* eyes?" said Isaac.

"Yes, five eyes, two large compound and three simple ones in-between," explained his grandfather.

"Wow!" said Isaac.

"As I was saying," said Mrs. Willowkins, "Norman paused for his five eyes to adjust to the dim light and spotted a long-legged spider hanging upside-down in a messy, tangled web…"

"No, sir, my house positively isn't ablaze," Norman clarified. "The fact of the matter is I've been called to go tell the Good News of

Jesus Christ to a hurting world, and I must hurry home to make preparations."

"Who called?" said the spider.

"The Lord God, Maker of heaven and earth," said Norman.

"So where you goin'," said the spider, "and how will you get there?"

"Hmmm," said Norman. "I don't know. He didn't say."

"What's your name, sonny?" said the spider.

"Norman," said the little insect. "Norman Hyde."

"Well, Norman Hyde, it seems to me that you'd best hold your horses till the Almighty tells you what to do next. I 'spect you just might need some gettin' ready and settin' before you skedaddle and go," said the old spider. "Remember, God called Moses to be a deliverer, but first trained him for forty long years on the back side of a sweltering desert."

"But I don't have forty years," Norman insisted. "We mantises only live *one* year – fourteen months at the most."

"Still, you'd do well to listen to Pappy Longlegs and wait for the Lord," the spider maintained. "You know what they say, 'the Lord is good to those who wait for Him.'"

"Maybe you're right," said Norman. "Maybe I ought to go home and pray instead of go home and pack. Thank you, Pappy Longlegs, for your wise advice. Good day, now."

"Anytime, sonny, anytime," said the spider. "See ya later alliga…uh, Norman."

Even by way of the musty crawl space, it took Norman till mid-afternoon to get to the myrtle tree and another thirty minutes to climb home. On home branch, he tucked his foreleg under his chin and bowed his tiny head.

"Thank You, Lord Jesus," he prayed, "for calling a slowpoke bug like me to go tell a hurting world about You. Now, Lord, I'd be much obliged if You'll tell me where to go and how to get there. Amen."

Norman sat very still on the smooth bark and waited for the Lord's answer. The lavender blossoms smelled sweet in the bright sunshine, and puffy, cotton clouds on a baby blue sky floated overhead. He waited and waited and waited and waited until the ruby red sun dropped under the far riverbank and a round moon rose behind him. Unable to keep one ear alert (yep, just one according to scientists) and five eyes open a minute longer, the little, brown mantis fell asleep.

In the early morning twilight, a clanging bell woke the insect. He yawned and blinked his eyes. Norman watched twin beams dance over the Coosa current as the river ferry moved slowly along a cable toward the church.

An old ferry boat run by the Chancellor family since the 1860s had transported passengers, horse-drawn wagons, and in Norman's day, automobiles, back and forth across the Coosa River between

Childersburg and Harpersville. The insect's favorite uncle, Jack, claimed that William McKinley, the 25th U.S. President, once rode that ferry while canvassing the great state of Alabama - and it must be so since Jack Hyde knew practically every Chancellor Ferry tale worth tattling in Talladega and Shelby County.

    The little, brown bug sat up straighter than an army soldier standing at attention. "Chancellor Ferry!" he shouted. "That's my where-to-go-and-how-to-get-there answer! Thank You, Lord Jesus! Undoubtedly, You're sending me to the far away land of Shelby County by way of the Chancellor Ferry to tell a hurting world Your Good News. I must tell Pappy Longlegs at once."

REFLECTIONS

POINTS to PONDER

1. Who did Norman meet under the church?
   _____

2. What was Pappy Longlegs' wise advice for Norman? _____ for the Lord's instructions.

God's PROMISE to you:

"Yet I am confident I will see the Lord's goodness while I am here in the land of the living. Wait patiently for the Lord. Be brave and courageous. Yes, wait patiently for the Lord." (Psalm 27:13-14)

(Hidden PEN POINT)

(A Bible verse. Lamentations 3:25 from the New King James Version: "The Lord is good to those who wait for Him, to the soul who seeks Him.")

Can you find the hidden PEN POINT in chapter 3?

Chapter 3
Go!

"Papaw, our cabin's on Chancellor Ferry Cove. Did the ferry dock here?" said Jacob.

"Nearby, hot rod," said Mr. Willowkins. "You know where the boat ramp sits right past the neighbors?"

"Yes, sir," said Jacob.

"Well, the old landing was just the other side of the boat ramp."

"Cool," Jacob, Elizabeth, and Isaac chimed together.

"Coo!" echoed little Alexander.

Everyone laughed.

"So, did Norman get on the ferry?" asked Elizabeth.

"Keep listenin', dear, and you'll find out," said Mrs. Willowkins. "Norman couldn't wait to tell his new friend the plan…"

"Pappy Longlegs, Pappy Longlegs, I know where I'm going and how to get there," Norman called after a vigorous hour's hike through the crawl space.

"What's that you're saying, sonny?" answered the old spider.

Norman leaned toward the shadowy corner and hollered, "I said I know where I'm going on mission and how to get there – Shelby

County by way of the Chancellor Ferry to tell a hurting world the Good News of Jesus."

"Well, that's just fine and dandy, Norman, fine and dandy indeed. So what's your itinerary?" said the spider.

"My I-what-a-rary?" Norman said.

"Your itinerary. You know, your timetable, travel plans, your schedule for the journey," said Pappy Longlegs.

"Oh, my itinerary is right now, straightaway, not a minute to waste. I'm headed to the landing this very moment," said Norman, "and simply stopped in to bid my goodbyes."

"Hold on now, Norman. That ferry boat's long gone since this morning's run, and there's no tellin' when it'll be back."

"Oh," sighed Norman. "I didn't think of that."

"Son, a mission's kinda like a recipe. You have your ingredients – that's where you're goin' – and your instructions – that's what to do when you get there – but you've also got to know the timin' – the *when* of the assignment," said the spider.

Norman sat quietly in the dirt looking lower than a bucket at the bottom of a dry well.

"What's the matter, sonny?" asked Pappy Longlegs.

"I'm too slow," muttered Norman. "Even if I start out as soon as the ferry leaves Harpersville, I'll never make it to the landing in time to get on board."

"*I'm* too slow, even if *I*, *I'll* never - what's all this talk about *I*," said the old spider. "Seems to me if the Lord did the callin', He'll see to it that you finish the chore. Son, you need to be a lookin' at God, not yourself, and trustin' Him."

Pappy's encouragement rekindled Norman's grit.

"You're right, Pappy Longlegs. Right as rain. God *is* faithful, and surely He'll make a way. I will trust Him with all my heart and not depend on my own understanding," said Norman. "Thank you, sir, and good day to you."

"After while crocod…uh, Norman," said the spider.

Norman took four steps and then whirled back around. "Pappy, a marvelous idea just sprang to my brain."

"What's that?" said the spider.

"If I depart immediately, I can camp along the way until I reach the river. Then I'll be ready to board the Chancellor Ferry whenever it does arrive," said Norman.

Pappy Longlegs grinned a toothless grin. "You could at that, my boy," he said. "You certainly could at that. Sounds to me like you've got the whole recipe now – the where, the how, *and* the when."

"Wish me well, Pappy Longlegs. I'm off to tell a hurting world the Good News of Jesus," said Norman. "Farewell, my friend."

Pappy waved a long, slender leg and called, "Happy trails to you, Norman."

Norman walked and walked and finally emerged from under the church house into the noonday heat. Exercising his good sense of direction, the determined, little mantis turned northwest and began the long journey to the ferry landing. He scaled clumps of bear grass, hopped over patches of sundried clay, and then spread his brown wings for a brief flight ending in the shade of a large oak tree beside the river road. The bug felt quite satisfied with his progress and decided to rest a spell. Unbeknownst to Norman, however, the hungry Mr. Robin Redbreast perched on a limb just above the vulnerable insect's tiny head, secretly watching his every move.

REFLECTIONS

POINTS to PONDER

1. How did Norman hope to get to Harpersville in Shelby County? By way of the Chancellor _____.
2. Pappy Longlegs told Norman that it's important to know God's _____ or *when* He wants you to do something.

God's PROMISE to you:

"For everything there is a season, a time for every activity under heaven...Yet God has made everything beautiful for its own time."
(Ecclesiastes 3:1,11a)

(Hidden PEN POINT)

(Another Bible verse. Proverbs 3:5 New Living Translation: "Trust in the Lord with all your heart, and do not depend on your own understanding.")

Can you find the hidden PEN POINT in chapter 4?

Chapter 4
Peter

"Oh, no!" cried Elizabeth.

"Ah, Lizzie, you know Norman's not gonna get eaten," said Jacob. "Mamaw's stories *always* have a happy ending."

"Not this one," teased their uncle. "The bird eats Norman, and then a big storm comes and sinks the ferry."

"He's just kidding, dears," Mrs. Willowkins assured her wide-eyed grandchildren. "Without so much as a chirp of warning...."

The famished bird made a beeline dive for the defenseless bug, but unexpectedly darted left and flew away. Norman looked up just in time to see Mr. Redbreast's tail feathers vanish through the treetops and then back down to discover ten bare toes wiggling within inches of his shady resting spot.

"A praying mantis," said Peter.

"Uh-oh," groaned Norman.

Nine-year-old Peter Weatherby had left the farm at dawn with a basket in one hand and a cane pole in the other and hitched a ride with Walter Chancellor across the Coosa River.

"I'll be back 'bout noontide to pick you up, Peter," Mr. Chancellor had promised. "That'll give you plenty of time to deliver those eggs and try your luck at fishing."

At the store, the boy didn't trade the fresh farm eggs for candy; instead, he bartered with Mr. Dunlap for much-needed groceries. The kind-hearted storekeeper swapped Peter's goods for generous portions of cornmeal, flour, salt, sugar, lard, and three peppermint sticks to boot – one for Peter, one for little Alice, and another for baby Ella. On the long hike back to the riverbank, Norman had caught his eye.

Peter scooped up the insect and held it close to his freckled face. "What happened to your leg?" he said. "Poor thing. Don't worry; I'll take care of you."

He grabbed a quart jar from his threadbare knapsack, stuffed grass, green leaves, twigs, and Norman into the jar, and then twisted closed the hole-punched lid.

"Now," said Peter, "let's go fishin'."

The boy whistled happily as he skipped down the road, but Norman, trapped in the Mason-jar jungle, didn't feel cheery by any stretch of the imagination. He pulled his foreleg under his chin, tightly closed five eyes, and earnestly prayed, "Have mercy upon me, O Lord, for I am in troub...Wait a minute."

Norman's attitude made an abrupt about-face. His circumstances appeared truly dreadful, but on the contrary, his situation might be a blessing.

He raised a leg over his head and bellowed, "Hallelujah! Praise the Lord! Thank You, Lord Jesus, for supplying a slowpoke bug with a speedy ride to the river to go tell a hurting world about You."

Remembering Pappy Longlegs' wise recommendation, he added, "And I'd be much obliged if You'll show me what to do when I get there. Amen."

Peter and Norman arrived at the Coosa in what seemed like only a few, short steps more than a hop, skip, and a jump – a trip that would have taken a dawdling bug days and days. Because a mantis occupied his worm jar, the boy searched the riverbank until he found a rusty tin can. Peter filled it with dirt and set it on the ground beside Norman. Next, using a large rock as a hammer, he drove a sturdy stick into the earth.

"Do you know how to fiddle for worms, buggy?" Peter said. "Watch this."

Norman pressed all eyes against the glass and watched the boy vigorously rub the rock back and forth, back and forth across the top of the stick, making it vibrate. In five shakes, an earthworm poked its head above ground and then another one and another and another.

"Amazing!" said Norman.

Peter stuck a wiggly worm on his hook, pitched the others in the old can, and then cast his line into the river.

"You hungry?" said Peter. "I am."

The boy pulled a half biscuit wrapped in a crumpled handkerchief from a pocket of his overalls and took a bite. When a fly buzzed by, Peter snatched it from the air with his free hand and tossed it into the Mason jar.

"Wow!" Norman said and then thanked the Lord for a delicious meal. "And, Lord Jesus, please help the human-child catch lots of fish to feed his hungry family. Amen."

REFLECTIONS

POINTS to PONDER

1. Who found Norman? _____
2. Norman's capture turned out to be a _____ instead of a problem.

God's PROMISE to you:

"And we know that God causes everything to work together for the good of those who love God and are called according to His purpose for them." (Romans 8:28)

(Hidden PEN POINT)

(Simon PETER was a fisherman. Jesus chose him and his brother, Andrew, as two of His twelve disciples. Peter was one of Jesus's best friends, and he wrote two books of the New Testament.)

(Read Luke 5:1-11)

Can you find the hidden PEN POINT in chapter 5?

Chapter 5
The Club

Isaac asked excitedly, "Papaw, can we piddle for worms tomorrow?"

"*F*iddle, not *p*iddle," said Elizabeth.

"Can we, Papaw?" said Isaac.

"We can try. Your great-granddaddy Willowkins was a top-notch fisherman, and he hunted worms that way."

"Did Peter catch a fish?" said Jacob.

"Sure as shootin'. No sooner had Norman said, 'Amen,' than Peter's bobber disappeared in the murky water," said Mrs. Willowkins…

"Got one!" Peter yelled.

"Thank You, Lord Jesus!" Norman shouted. "Keep the line tight, child."

The boy pulled in a hand-sized bream.

Norman prayed, "Please, Lord, send a boat full."

When the ferry docked at high noon, Peter held up the homemade stringer sporting two catfish, four bream, three crappies, and a large striped bass.

"Look, Mr. Chancellor," called Peter excitedly. "Ain't they beauties!"

Mr. Chancellor hooted. "Would you look at that! Now there's some fine eatin', Peter - mighty fine. Hurry up, boy, and get your things. Your pop's lookin' for you."

"Yes, sir," Peter said and hurriedly snatched the cane pole, knapsack, stringer, and Norman's jar and ran to the ferry.

"Whatcha got in the jar?" said Mr. Chancellor.

"I found me a mantis," said Peter proudly. "He's only got five legs, but I figure on keepin' him for a pet. Pop told me not to bring home anymore critters to feed, but a bug-eatin' bug ought a be okay; don't you think?"

Mr. Chancellor laughed. "I reckon so. Hold on tight, Peter. Here we go."

Oh, how I wish Pappy Longlegs could see me now, Norman marveled. *Slowpoke Norman Hyde onboard the Chancellor Ferry headed to Shelby County to tell the Good News of Jesus to a hurting world in only a half-day's time. Lord, with You all things certainly are possible!*

Overjoyed, Norman sang a hymn he'd learned from the windowsill:

"On Jordan's stormy banks I stand, and cast a wishful eye

To Canaan's fair and happy land, where my possessions lie.

I am bound for the PROMISED LAND, I am bound for the PROMISED LAND;

O who will come and go with me? I am bound for the PROMISED LAND."

"Thanks, Mr. Chancellor," Peter said when they touched the far bank. "See you later."

Peter galloped away, gripping the Mason jar in one fist. Norman's head spun from juddering up and down, up and down, up and down like cream in a butter churn, and his first view of Shelby County was merely a blur.

Oh my, thought Norman, *perhaps I'm not cut out to go tell a hurting world about Jesus after all. Perhaps I should go back to my sweet myrtle tree.*

The little, brown insect imagined Pappy's crackly voice utter, "*I'm* not, *I* should...what's all this talk about *I*. Son, you need to be a lookin' at God, not yourself, and a trustin' Him."

Norman shook his head, blinked his eyes, adjusted his outlook, and braced himself for the wild ride. The boy didn't slow up a minute until he neared a footpath to "The Club."

"Now, children, don't go picturing some fancy, highfalutin country club where menfolk played golf and womenfolk sipped tea and gossiped," said Mrs. Willowkins. "No indeed. That old place was nothing but a tumbledown log shack leaning on a cracked, rock chimney."

"The chimney's still standing on the riverbank," Mr. Willowkins added.

"Sure is," said Mrs. Willowkins. "The Club roosted in-between the Chancellors and Weatherbys - about a half-mile down river from Mr. Chancellor's farm and a quarter-mile upstream from Tom Weatherby's place. Too many brothers out of money and short on hope crawled to that haunt in the dark of the night like roaches to a trash heap to drown their sorrows in moonshine whiskey and flirt with lady luck around the gambling tables…"

Peter's mama had threatened to skin him alive if she ever caught him anywhere near that devil's den. Sometimes a boy's curiosity can pull him straight opposite of good sense, but to this point, Peter had minded and stayed away – up to this point, that is.

All alone on a deserted dirt road with nobody watching but Norman's five eyes, the boy commenced to figuring that a quick sneak-peak of that hangout might just help him understand why he wasn't supposed to go there. He glanced here. He glanced there. Presuming the coast was clear, he slithered down the forbidden path, but around the first bend of the trail, as Providence would have it, he ran right smack dab into Tom Weatherby – Peter's pop.

REFLECTIONS

POINTS to PONDER

1. Peter's mother told him to never go near The _____.
2. When he thought no one was watching, Peter decided to _____ his mother.

God's PROMISE to you:

"Children, obey your parents because you belong to the Lord, for this is the right thing to do." (Ephesians 6:1)

(Hidden PEN POINT)

(PROMISED LAND is the land God promised to give His children, the Israelites. He first made the promise to Abraham. The land extended from the Negev wilderness in the south to the Lebanon mountains in the north and from the Euphrates River in the east to the Mediterranean Sea in the west.)

(Read Genesis 12:1-2 and Joshua 1:2-4)

Can you find the hidden PEN POINT in chapter 6?

Chapter 6
Prayer Pals

"I know that feeling," said little Alexander and baby Hunter's dad. "I remember in middle school asking Mama how she always knew when I did something wrong."

"What'd she say?" said Mr. Willowkins.

"She said God told her."

"He did," declared Mrs. Willowkins. "The Lord loved you enough to stop you, just like Peter's dad stopped him. Mr. Weatherby put a calloused hand on his son's shoulder and boomed…"

"Peter Thomas Weatherby, where do you think you're going?"

*Where have **you** been?* Peter wondered, but he knew better than to ask.

"Uh, uh, I was…uh…I was comin' to show you these fish, Pop. Aren't they fine?" Peter stammered and then held up his catch.

Mr. Weatherby's face softened, and he reached for the heavy stringer.

"They sure are, son," he said. "Come on. We've got chores to do."

"And look, Pop. I found a five-legged praying mantis," Peter said. "I reckon this pet won't cost a penny to feed."

Mr. Weatherby smiled – something Peter wished he'd do more often – and said, "Nope, nary a penny. We've got more than enough flies to spare."

At the farm, Peter's mother stood in the blazing sun clipping sheets to a clothesline stretched between steel poles. Five-year-old Alice and baby Ella played on a patchwork quilt in the nearby shade. The little girls were enjoying an imaginary birthday party.

"Here's another piece of cake, baby Ella," little Alice said. "Isn't it delicious? I made it myself."

Baby Ella clapped her chubby hands and pretended to take a bite of the invisible delicacy.

Neither Peter nor Tom admitted to Abby Weatherby where they'd "happened" to run into each other. But after the tasty fried fish and cornbread supper and washing the dirty dishes, Peter knelt by his cot and confessed to God.

"Lord Jesus, I'm real sorry for disobeyin' Mama and headin' for The Club today. Please forgive me. And the next time I step into temptation, Lord, please help me hold the line. Please bless Mama and Pop and little Alice and baby Ella. Things sure are tough for my pop, Lord, - trying to feed a family of five in these hard times. Would You help him, too, please, and turn his heart toward You? And if it's not too much trouble, would You help Mama not worry so much. Amen."

"Amen," said Norman.

Peter set the Mason jar in the open window beside his narrow bed. "Good night, buggy," he said sleepily.

"Good night, Peter," said Norman.

Minutes later, the little, brown mantis heard the boy's deep, steady breathing and knew he was fast asleep. Norman surveyed the cloudless sky above his glass house. A full, silver ball on the star-spangled stage sketched moon shadows over the farmyard. He saw a mouse scurry under the barn door and listened to the cricket and katydid orchestra perform liberty's rhapsody.

Norman sighed. "Lord, how will an imprisoned, slowpoke mantis ever tell a hurting world about You from the limiting confines of a Mason jar?"

Pappy Longlegs' hopeful counsel again overpowered Norman's woebegone disposition. "Seems to me, if the Lord did the callin', He'll see to it that the job gets done. Son, you need to trust in God."

Peter and Norman were out of bed and in the kitchen before the next day's sunlight kissed the horizon. Mrs. Weatherby set two boiled eggs and a glass of buttermilk in front of her boy.

"Don't forget to say grace," she said.

Norman immediately slipped a leg under his chin and bowed his head.

"Look, Mama," Peter said, "he's praying!"

Mrs. Weatherby peered in the jar. "Well, Mr. Mantis, say an extra prayer for the Weatherbys today, please. We sure need it."

"I most certainly will, Mrs. Weatherby," Norman promised.

Peter thanked the Lord for breakfast, and Norman fervently recited the Lord's Prayer. "Dear Father God, which art in heaven, holy be Thy name. May Thy kingdom come and Thy will be done on earth, as it is in heaven. Please give the Weatherbys and me our daily bread, and forgive us our sins as we forgive those who sin against us. Let us not yield to temptations, but deliver us from evil. For Thine, O Lord, is the kingdom, and the power, and the glory forever."

"Amen," said Norman and Peter simultaneously.

REFLECTIONS

POINTS to PONDER

1. What did Peter and Norman do when they made a mistake or needed help? They _____
2. Prayer is simply talking to God. Do you talk to God? YES   NO

God's PROMISE to you:

"Don't worry about anything; instead, pray about everything. Tell God what you need, and thank Him for all He has done." (Philippians 4:6)
"In those days when you pray, I will listen...I will be found by you," says the Lord. (Jeremiah 29:12,14a)

(Hidden PEN POINT)

(The LORD'S PRAYER. One day, Jesus was in a certain place praying. When He finished, a disciple said, "Lord, teach us to pray." Jesus then taught His friends an example of how believers should pray.)

(Read Luke 11:1-4)

Can you find the hidden PEN POINT in chapter 7?

Chapter 7
On the Farm

Baby Lee squirmed in Mrs. Willowkins' arms and started fussing.

"Here, Miss Martha, I'll take him," said his mother. "It's time for his bottle."

Mrs. Willowkins kissed the soft, round head, handed the baby to her daughter-in-law, and resumed the story.

"After feeding the chickens, two milk cows, and Oscar, the plow mule…"

Peter carried a hoe and the Mason jar to the vegetable garden, and to Norman's delight, the boy opened the lid to let the little mantis explore while he weeded long rows of wilted silver queen corn and snap beans. When a yellow jacket landed near his new friend's bare foot, the insect ambushed the wasp with surprising speed and used his front leg's spines to keep a firm grip. He devoured the foe in a wink.

"Woo-hoo!" roared Norman.

The mantis found country life invigorating having lived all his born days in the lavender myrtle tree beside Mt. Olive Missionary Baptist Church in the small town of Childersburg. He prayed, "Thank You, Lord Jesus, for calling a slowpoke bug to this farm in Shelby

County and solving two problems in one skirmish - sparing Peter from a painful sting and filling my empty belly for the day."

"Pete," Mr. Weatherby called.

"Yes, sir?" Peter answered.

"Come help me mend the fence when you're done in the garden."

"Yes, sir," Peter said.

"Some children, nowadays, complain if they have to carry a paper plate to the wastebasket after a microwaved lunch," noted Mrs. Willowkins. "But Peter liked working on the farm – especially alongside his papa…"

Peter held the boards Mr. Weatherby nailed to the posts and sang boisterously. Norman joined in on the chorus:

"To the work! To the work! Let the hungry be fed;

To the fountain of life let the thirsty be led;

In the CROSS and its vict'ry our glory shall be,

While we herald the tidings, "Salvation is free!"

"Work for Him by His grace;

Work through Him for His praise;

Work with Him all the days;

And work in Him in many ways."

Next, the boy scrubbed the kitchen floor with a corncob mop and shoveled manure from the barn stalls. After a cornbread and buttermilk lunch, he built a fire to heat Mrs. Weatherby's wash water.

"Peter," Mrs. Weatherby said.

"Yes 'am," he answered.

"Those sure were good fish last night. You think you and your new friend can find a bullfrog or two down at the creek this afternoon?"

"Yes, ma'am!" Peter said happily.

The boy threw Norman's jar in his knapsack and trotted across the cotton fields, into the woods, and down a soft, pine straw paved path to Morgan Creek. Rainless July days had shriveled the babbling brook to a slow stream.

"Buggy, you better stay inside your jar down here," said Peter, "so you don't get eat up by a bird or a snake or some other starvin' critter."

Peter put fresh leaves in Norman's house. He set it beside a river birch and waded into the cool water.

"Croakers love hidin' behind the falls," Peter explained.

The boy grasped under a cascade. On the first try, he pulled out a brownish, olive-green bullfrog with large, protruding eyes and long, sturdy hind legs.

"Remarkable," said Norman.

Peter collected three more frogs and then plopped down beside Norman.

"See those clouds building over yonder and feel that breeze?" Peter said. "That means rain's comin'. We better go home.

Drop.

Drip.

I believe Peter is the smartest nine-year-old in the whole state of Alabama, thought Norman.

Drop.

Drip-drop.

Drip-drop-drip.

The pitter-patter of raindrops rapidly sped to a downpour.

Peter danced through the cotton shrubs and sang:

"It's raining; it's pouring.

The old man is snoring.

He went to bed and bumped his head.

And he wouldn't get up till morning."

REFLECTIONS

POINTS to PONDER

1. On the farm, Peter _____ before he played.
2. Did Peter complain about his chores?   YES   NO

God's PROMISE to you:

"Work willingly at whatever you do, as though you were working for the Lord rather than for people. Remember that the Lord will give you an inheritance as your reward, and that the Master you are serving is Christ." (Colossians 3:23-24)

(Hidden PEN POINT)

(The CROSS - God's Son, Jesus Christ, died on a large, wooden cross to take the punishment for people's sins. For those who trust in Him, His wonderful work on the cross saves them, delivers them, forgives their sins, and freely gives them never-ending, eternal life.)
(Read Phil. 2:5-11 and Eph. 1:6-8)

Can you find the hidden PEN POINT in chapter 8?

Chapter 8
Peter's Burning Question

Mrs. Willowkins said, "Over their mouthwatering, frog-leg supper..."

"Ooooo!" groaned the wee-Willowkins.

"They ate *frog* legs!" said Jacob.

Mr. Willowkins laughed. "Sure! Tastes just like chicken."

"As I was saying," said Mrs. Willowkins. "Over the mouthwatering, frog-leg supper..."

Mr. Weatherby maintained that a stroke of good luck brought the much-needed rain, but Peter held other suspicions. He wondered if a full string of fish, a bulging sack of bullfrogs, and a soaking rainstorm after a month's drought – all in one week's time – might just possibly have something to do with the little, brown praying mantis in the Mason jar.

I'm gonna ask Pastor Titus next Sunday, he thought.

Sundays won first place as Peter's favorite day of the week. Abby Weatherby insisted that her family observe a Sabbath rest, and Tom Weatherby didn't argue.

"For six days shalt thou labor, and do thy work, but on the seventh day is the Sabbath of the Lord thy God: in it thou shalt not do any work, thou, nor thy son, nor thy daughter," she quoted from the Ten Commandments.

On Norman's very first Sunday at the farm, Peter hid the jar under his tattered Bible in the knapsack and then held little Alice's hand the three-quarter-mile walk to the ferry landing. Mr. Chancellor gave free rides to churchgoers, and Abby, Peter, Alice, and baby Ella were regular passengers.

"Lord," prayed Norman, "thank You for another Sabbath rest and the opportunity to visit Childersburg again. Please bless the Weatherbys and help Mr. Weatherby follow You. Lord, I pray he'll join the family at church soon. In Jesus name I pray. Amen."

From the sack, Norman heard Pastor Titus' familiar voice rumble, "Ladies and gentlemen, boys and girls..."

And bugs, thought Norman.

"Jesus said, 'If ye have faith as a grain of a mustard seed, ye shall say unto this mountain, remove hence to yonder place, and it shall remove!'"

"Amen," cheered Norman.

"And nothing shall be impossible unto you!"

"Hallelujah!" Norman cheered once more.

The boy liked Titus Koonce. His kind eyes and broad smile made his parishioners feel they mattered to God and their pastor. Every Sunday after the morning message, the preacher stood at the front door warmly shaking hands. Peter normally bolted from the pew to play tag with the other boys in the churchyard, but today, he lingered toward the rear of the line mustering the courage to ask his burning question.

"Howdy, preacher," he said at his turn and shook the large hand.

"Good morning, Peter. How are you today, and how are things on the farm?" said Pastor Titus.

"I'm good, thank you, and we had an extra good week at the farm, too," said Peter. "Uh, Pastor Titus, I've got...I've got a question."

"What's that, son?" said Pastor Titus.

Peter dropped the knapsack by his feet and pulled out the glass jar and Norman. "I found a mantis this week," he said. "He's only got five legs."

The pastor took the jar and looked at Norman. "Oh, he's a fine one."

"He's a *praying* mantis, you know," said Peter.

"Yes, I see that," said Pastor Titus.

"Well, it's like this, pastor. Ever since I found this praying mantis, good things have been happenin' – like catchin' a big mess of fish and a sack full of bullfrogs, and on top of that, we even got a soakin' rain on our garden that was drier than the desert."

"Praise the Lord," said the pastor.

"It seems to me like ever'time I pray, this here bug bows its head, too," said Peter. "Preacher, can bugs pray?"

"First, let me say that I'm very happy to hear *you're* praying, Peter. And about this mantis, well, like they say, the Good Lord sometimes works in mysterious ways," said Pastor Titus. "God tells us many things, but some of His mysteries we just can't understand. Deuteronomy 29:29 says 'the *secret* things belong to the LORD our God, but those things which are *revealed* belong unto us and to our children forever, that we may do all the words of this law.'"

"What does that mean?" asked Peter.

"Well, son, God doesn't tell us everything. Some things are purely His secrets. But if we'll faithfully obey what He clearly tells us in His law - the Bible - we know plenty enough to keep us busy all the days of our lives. Like love one another, be ye kind one to another, forgive others as your heavenly Father has forgiven you, rejoice always, give thanks in all circumstances, and pray without ceasing - just to name a few."

"But what about all them good things that happened last week?" said Peter.

"Just tell God thank You. The Bible says that every good and perfect gift is from Him," said Pastor Titus. "Always remember, Peter, it's not who's praying that matters as much as *who* we're praying to, and tell your father that I'm praying to Jesus for him."

REFLECTIONS

POINTS to PONDER

1. Pastor Titus told Peter that it matters _____ we pray to.
2. Pastor Titus prayed to _____ for Mr. Weatherby.

God's PROMISE to you:

"Keep on asking...Keep on seeking...Keep on knocking. For everyone who asks, receives. Everyone who seeks, finds. And to everyone who knocks, the door will be opened...So if you sinful people know how to give good gifts to your children, how much more will your heavenly Father give good gifts to those who ask Him." (Matthew 7:7-11)

(Hidden PEN POINT)

(The TEN COMMANDMENTS – are a set of biblical principles or laws that God inscribed on two stone tablets and gave to Moses on Mount Sinai.)

(Read Exodus 20:1-17)

Can you find the hidden PEN POINT in chapter 9?

Chapter 9
Cumulonimbus Picnic

"Martha's an answered prayer," declared Mr. Willowkins. "When I was sixteen, I asked Jesus to show me the girl I was gonna marry, and two weeks later, I met your grandmother at a church whiffle ball game. But I had to ask her three times to marry me before she said yes."

Mr. Willowkins leaned over and firmly kissed his bride of thirty-nine years.

Mrs. Willowkins blushed. "Well, the first two times I was only a girl. But the third time I was a senior in college and said yes faster than you can say…"

"Wilbur Willowkins wore a winter weskit," recited their children in unison.

"Now, back to the story," said Mrs. Willowkins. "Norman pressed his tiny face against the jar and tapped the glass…"

"Excuse me, Pastor Titus," he said, "I also have a question, please. How does a mantis in a Mason jar go about telling a hurting world the Good News of Jesus Christ?"

Pastor Titus tapped back. "Hey little fellow. You and Peter keep knocking on heaven's doors with those prayers. The Lord God promises that He listens in those days when we pray."

"But, sir, that doesn't answer my question," Norman said. *If only the humankind understood buggish language*, he thought.

Peter held the Mason jar on the boat railing during the ferry ride home, giving Norman a marvelous view of the historical Coosa River. In past centuries, Hernando de Soto had explored its shores, and Creek and Cherokee Native Americans had dwelt along the riverbanks. Sadly, the Creeks and Cherokees were forcibly removed, which left the Coosa River Valley wide open for American settlers and cotton farmers. Peter's great-grandfather, Josiah Weatherby, was among those early farmers and had cleared and worked the very land Tom Weatherby now farmed. When Abby, Peter, Alice, Ella, and Norman got back to the farm, however, Mr. Weatherby was nowhere to be found, and Peter noticed the cloud of worry over his mother's pretty face.

"Mama," he said, "let's have a picnic down by the creek today. I'll help you get things ready. The girls 'll love it."

Little Alice jumped up and down, squealing, "A picnic! A picnic!" and Baby Ella giggled.

"A picnic would be nice," said Mrs. Weatherby. "Peter, go pick a melon from the garden and fetch the pull cart from the barn. Alice, get Granny Weatherby's quilt from the chifforobe, and I'll fry croquettes from a can of salmon I've been saving. Yes, an outing will be good for all of us."

Sooner than you can say 'Sabbath Sunday family fun', mother and children packed the cart and paraded down the pine straw lane to Morgan Creek. A steady breeze through the tall pines and the sun's game of hide and seek behind swollen cumulonimbus clouds gave a welcomed reprieve from the long heat wave. A chipmunk momentarily joined the caravan before disappearing under a moss-covered log, and a cherry red cardinal chirped a merry tune from a nearby sweet gum limb.

Baby Ella pointed. "Bir," she cooed.

After lunch, Norman watched his new family through the Mason glass. Peter and little Alice frolicked in the creek like well-fed calves let out to pasture, and Baby Ella slept peacefully beside her mother. Mrs. Weatherby dipped her feet in the refreshing water and read a psalm aloud from the heavy *King James Bible* across her knees: "Delight thyself also in the Lord: and He shall give thee the desires of thine heart. Commit thy way unto the Lord; trust also in Him; and He shall bring it to pass. And He shall bring forth thy righteousness as the light, and thy judgment as the noonday. Rest in the Lord, and wait patiently for Him."

A loud clap of thunder abruptly interrupted their lovely afternoon. Like the chipmunk under the mossy log, the sun vanished behind dark, threatening clouds, and the gentle breeze morphed to a stiff wind.

"Quick, Peter," Mrs. Weatherby said, "a storm's brewin'. Help me pack the wagon."

Peter and Alice scrambled out of the water. Mrs. Weatherby hurriedly stacked tin plates and cups in the picnic basket, and Peter threw it in the cart. Suddenly, a burst of wind whipped through the treetops, and a strange noise rattled the woods.

"Hailstorm! Peter, get Ella," Mrs. Weatherby cried and whisked Alice into her arms.

Peter snatched his baby sister from the quilt, and the startled toddler began to cry.

"Leave the cart. Here, grab the quilt and put it over our heads. Run. Run to the barn as fast as you can," their mother ordered. "The house is too far away."

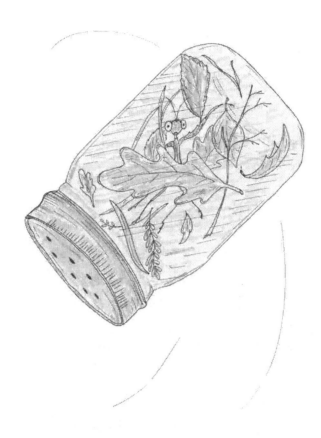

Norman sat dumbfounded in the Mason jar that just happened to be sitting on Granny Weatherby's double-wedding-ring quilt. When Peter jerked the cover from the ground, Norman and jar went airborne. Up, up, up he flew and down, down, down he tumbled - hitting the earth with a crushing thud. Norman heard shattering glass, and then all fell black and silent.

REFLECTIONS

POINTS to PONDER

1. When Mr. Weatherby wasn't home, Mrs. Weatherby looked _____. What do *you* worry about?
   _____

2. At the picnic, Mrs. Weatherby read the _____.

God's PROMISE to you:

"O how I love Your law! It is my meditation all the day. Your commandments make me wiser...How sweet are Your words to my taste! Yes, sweeter than honey to my mouth! From Your precepts I get understanding...Your word is a lamp to my feet and a light to my path." (Psalm 119:97-105)

(Hidden PEN POINT)

(A PSALM is a sacred song or hymn. Many of the Old Testament sacred songs in the book of Psalms were written by King David, including Psalm 37:4-7 that Mrs. Weatherby read.)

Can you find the hidden PEN POINT in chapter 10?

Chapter 10
Well Done

Jacob grinned. "I'm the only grandkid with a baby sister."

"I'm not a baby!" said Elizabeth.

"I'm the oldest," said Jacob, "so that makes you a *baby*."

"Am not!" Elizabeth insisted.

"Are, too!" countered Jacob.

"Okay, guys, let Mamaw finish the story," said their mother. "I want to know what happens to the Weatherbys and Norman."

Mrs. Willowkins said, "Back at the farm house, poor Mr. Weatherby was in a dither…"

"Abby! Peter! Where are you?" Mr. Weatherby shouted frantically.

He picked up the washtub sitting on the back porch and sprinted to the barn under the metal umbrella. Quarter-size hail beat the tub like a kettledrum in the Alabama Symphony Orchestra.

"Alice! Ella!" he yelled.

The barn stood empty except for the milk cows and Cinnamon, the orange tabby cat. Mr. Weatherby slumped to his knees.

"Lord Jesus, please help me find my family. Where can they be?" he cried.

Morgan Creek! he thought. *Maybe they went down to the creek after church.*

Mr. Weatherby pulled the tub back over his head and dashed out the back barn door. "Help me, Lord. Please help me find 'em," he pleaded again. "I'm sorry. I'm sorry I deserted You when this awful depression hit. I'm sorry I went to The Club instead of goin' to church with Abby and the kids, and I'm so sorry I'm not with 'em right now. I wanna change – really change. From now on, I promise I'll live Your way, Lord. No more whiskey. No more gambling away hard-earned money. Please, help me find 'em, Lord. Please!"

Halfway across the cotton field, Mr. Weatherby heard Ella's wails above the pounding hail and spotted Granny Weatherby's quilt over four running legs scrambling toward him.

"Thank You, Lord Jesus! Thank You," Mr. Weatherby repeated over and over and over as he raced down the cotton row to his loved ones.

"Get under the tub!" he shouted.

He kissed his wife and swept little Alice and baby Ella into his strong arms. The baby hushed crying and nestled her curly head into Tom's broad shoulder. With Peter on his left and Abby on his right, five Weatherbys scampered to the barn.

Meanwhile, Norman opened his bright eyes to dazzling light and the most beautiful music he'd ever heard.

"Wow, that certainly was a short-lived storm," said Norman.

"Norman," Someone called.

"Yes," said Norman. "Here I am."

"Norman, come here."

The little mantis started toward the compelling Voice, and then froze. Flabbergasted, he spouted, "I have *six* legs! And I'm *silver* - pure silver – shiny as a new dime. I can't believe it. I have six legs."

Laughter like the sound of rushing waters rippled through the pure, clear air. "Yes, I know. Come to Me, Norman."

Norman skipped over the gilded cobblestones toward the Man with outstretched arms. The Figure was clothed in a white robe reaching to His feet that shone like burnished bronze when it's made to glow in the furnace, and a golden sash girded His chest. In His eyes, Norman saw love, which surpassed knowledge.

The little insect bowed low to the ground. "My Lord and Savior," said Norman. "I'm so sorry, dear Jesus."

"Why are you sorry, little one?" said the Lord.

"You sent me to go tell a hurting world Your Gospel Good News, and I failed," said Norman tearfully.

Jesus sat down beside a crystal river and gently lifted Norman to His knee.

"Well done, My good and faithful, little servant," He said.

"But Master, I didn't accomplish my mission. I never told the hurting world about You," said Norman.

"True. You never *told* hurting people about Me, but you know what?"

"What?" said Norman.

"You *served* a hurting family very well. Young Peter needed a friend, and you stuck closer than a brother. Abby ached for a miracle, and you prayed for the deepest longings of her heart. Tom needed an intercessor, and you stood in the gap – fervently pleading for him to trust Me and return to My church with his family. Norman, I answered your prayers. Tom repented in the hailstorm and committed to following Me from this day forward," said the Lord Jesus.

"Oh, thank You, Lord Jesus! Thank You! How marvelous are Your works. Your greatness is excellent and mighty are Your wonderful deeds. Let everything that has breath praise You, my God and my King," Norman worshiped.

"Norman, I hereby bestow upon you the title of Norman "Praying" Hyde of Chancellor Ferry - my faithful, little servant who obediently went forth and helped snatch a Coosa River family from the pit of despair during the Great Depression of the U.S. of A."

"So, children, now you know the link between the missionary, John "Praying" Hyde of India and the five-legged, little, brown mantis, Norman "Praying" Hyde of Alabama," said Mrs. Willowkins. "Both Mr. Hydes were faithful servants that shared God's love with hurting people."

By the time Mrs. Willowkins finished the story, Wilbur and all the wee Willowkins had fallen fast asleep – THE END of another happy day at the Willowkins' hunting cabin on the Harpersville bank of the Coosa River where the Chancellor Ferry crossed back and forth so many years ago.

REFLECTIONS

POINTS to PONDER

1. Mr. Weatherby repented of his sins and committed his life to _____. Have you given your life to Jesus? YES   NO
2. In heaven, the Lord Jesus applauded Norman for sharing God's _____ with others.

God's PROMISE to you:

"Jesus said, 'Don't let your hearts be troubled. Trust in God, and trust in Me....I am going to prepare a place for you. Whenever it is ready, I will come and get you, so that you will always be with Me where I am...I am the way, the truth, and the life.
No one can come to the Father except through Me.'" (John 14:1-6)
"Everyone who calls on the name of the Lord will be saved." (Romans 10:13)

(Hidden PEN POINT)

(The CRYSTAL RIVER – Scripture describes the River of Life in heaven as being as clear as crystal and coming from the throne of God and the Lamb.)
(Read Revelation 22:1)

AFTERWORD

Founded in the 1860s by William Chancellor, the Chancellor Ferry was in constant operation across the Coosa River between Harpersville and Childerburg, Alabama for some seventy years. Special thanks are extended to Barbara Adkins, the great, great granddaughter of William Chancellor, and David Dunlap, whose father owned Dunlap Grocery & Market on Highway 91 in Childersburg. Thank you for graciously sharing helpful information and family stories.

In 2012, my family purchased 60 acres along the Coosa near the old ferry landing and built a hunting cabin with a wrap-around porch so our grandchildren can run laps *outside* when it rains. ☺

(A secret PEN POINT: The characters of NORMAN Hyde and Pastor Titus KOONCE were named in honor of Mr. NORMAN KOONCE, a great man of God. Many, many years ago in a Sunday School class for newlyweds at the First Baptist Church in Bogalusa, Louisiana, Mr. Koonce used the Bible and captivating stories to teach us the value of personal, everyday relationship with Jesus and the importance of abiding in God's infinite love, Word, and power. Thank you, Mr. Koonce, for faithfully serving the Lord and sharing His truth.)

Made in the USA
Middletown, DE
25 March 2016